Farm Animals

Turkeys

Rachael Bell

Heinemann Library
Chicago, Illinois

Designed by AMR
Originated by Ambassador Litho
Printed in Hong Kong/China

04 03 02 01 00
10 9 8 7 6 5 4 3 2 1

Library of Congress Cataloging-in-Publication Data
Bell, Rachael.
    Turkeys / Rachael Bell.
        p. cm. – (Farm animals)
    Includes bibliographical references (p.) and index.
    Summary: Introduces this familiar farm animal by describing its physical appearance,
manner of reproduction, eating and roosting habits, ways of staying healthy, required
care, and uses.
    ISBN 1-57572-534-7 (lib. bdg.)
    1. Turkeys—Juvenile literature. [1. Turkeys.] I. Title.
SF507.B45 2000
636.5'92—dc21   99-043372
                                                   CIP

Acknowledgments
Agripicture/Peter Dean, p. 19; Anthony Blake Photo Library/Joy Skipper, pp. 13 & 25; Anthony Blake
Photo Library, pp. 22 (center), 25; British Turkey Information Service pp. 4, 11, 14, 22 (outside), 23, 26;
Corbis/Phil Schermeister, p. 17; Corbis/Raymond Gehman, p. 28; Holt Studios/Andrew Linscott, p. 15;
Chris Honeywell, p. 24; Images of Nature/FLPA/Gerard Lacz, p. 9; Images of Nature/FLPA/L. Lee Rue p.
18; Robert Kauffman, p 7; Rouse/Elliott Photographers, pp. 20, 21, 27; Lynn M. Stone pp. 8, 10, 12, 16, 29;
Tony Stone Images/Art Wolfe, p. 5; Tony Stone Images/Gary Moon, p. 6.

Cover photograph reproduced with permission of FLPA.

Our thanks to the American Farm Bureau Federation for their comments in the preparation
of this book.

Every effort has been made to contact copyright holders of any material reproduced in this
book. Any omissions will be rectified in subsequent printings if notice is given to the Publisher.

Some words are shown in bold, **like this.** You can find out what they mean by looking in the glossary.

Contents

Turkey Relatives

Turkeys are large birds that come in different colors and sizes. Most farmers keep white turkeys because they grow very quickly.

There are still wild turkeys at the edges of forests in many parts of the **Americas.** Wild turkeys are smaller than farm turkeys.

Welcome to the Farm

Farmers often **raise** more than one kind of animal. On this farm, there are turkeys and cows.

This farmer uses part of the land for raising turkeys. The rest of the farm land is used to grow **crops** and for cows to **graze** on.

Meet the Turkeys

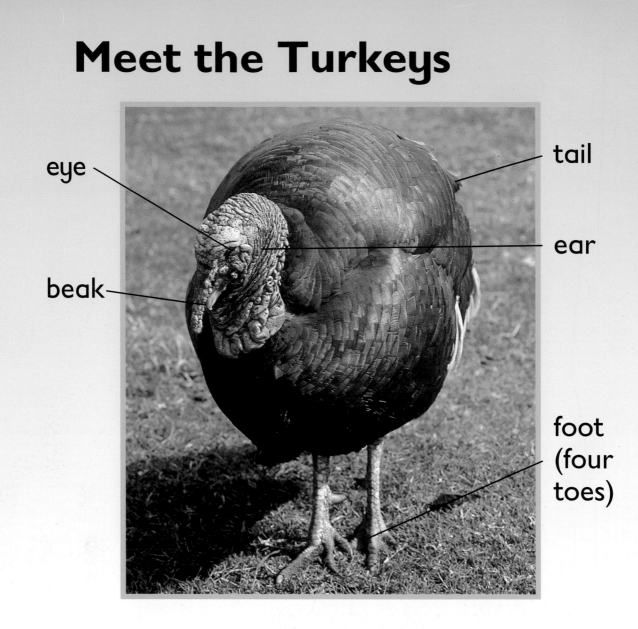

eye

tail

ear

beak

foot
(four
toes)

Female turkeys are called hens.
An adult hen can weigh as much
as a six-month-old baby!

snood   **wattle**   tail

caruncle   tassel   spur

Male turkeys are called toms. They are about twice as big as the hens. If they are upset, toms can make the skin flaps on their head stretch or change color.

Meet the Baby Turkeys

The hen lays eggs in the spring. She sits on her eggs for four weeks. Then the **poults** peck their way out of the shell. The poults are covered in **down.**

The poults are small enough to fit in your hand! Feathers grow in place of the down when the poults are about twelve days old.

Where Do Turkeys Live?

The **poults** stay under a heat lamp until they have feathers. Their box has round walls, so that they don't **huddle** in the corners.

When they are bigger, the turkeys live in a shed with straw on the floor to keep them clean and warm. They can go outside into a **pen.**

What Do Turkeys Eat?

When **poults** are inside their shells, they eat the **yolk** and egg white. After they **hatch,** they eat **starter crumbs** from a small **trough**.

When the turkeys are outside, they eat anything that is green. The farmer also feeds them special **pellets** and wheat. He gives them plenty of water to drink.

Staying Healthy

Turkeys raised on farms cannot fly. But they can run very fast! Running around their **pen** gives them plenty of exercise.

Turkeys **preen** to keep themselves clean. They flap dust over themselves, then shake it off. Dust baths help them stay cool.

How Do Turkeys Sleep?

Wild turkeys **roost** in trees at night to keep safe. They grip a branch with their feet, so that they don't fall off when they are asleep.

On the farm, turkeys go inside at
dusk. They puff out their feathers and
bend their neck. They sleep standing
on the straw.

Raising Turkeys

On this farm, the farmer and his family take care of the turkeys. The children see if the turkeys need more straw. The farmer gives the turkeys food and water.

The children help their father gather
the turkeys. Turkeys stay together.
If one turkey goes inside, the others
will follow.

How Are Turkeys Used?

Farmers raise turkeys because their meat is good to eat. It is very **lean** and easy to cook. It can be used in many different dishes.

Many people eat roast turkey at Thanksgiving. Turkey is a popular holiday food in the United States and Canada.

Large Turkey Farms

Large turkey farms **raise** thousands of turkeys. The meat is sent to supermarkets. The turkeys are wrapped in plastic and frozen.

On large farms, the turkeys are kept in big buildings. The farmer can take care of many turkeys at once. The buildings can be kept at just the right **temperature** for the turkeys.

More Turkey Farms

Some turkey farms just buy turkey eggs
and **hatch** them. They sell the **poults**
to other farmers. The other farmers
grow the poults to their adult size.

On these farms, machines **incubate** the eggs. That way they can hatch many hundreds of eggs. They can also check on all the poults as they hatch.

Fact File

 Poults grow very quickly. They can gain the same amount each day as they weighed when they **hatched.**

 When a hen is sitting on her eggs, she will not leave them. The farmer has to lift her off the eggs to feed her.

 Male turkeys are sometimes called "gobblers" because of the sound they make. This sound tells other males to stay away.

Benjamin Franklin was one of the men who helped start the U.S. government. He wanted the turkey to be the **national emblem** of the United States. He thought the turkey was a better choice for an emblem than the bald eagle.

When turkeys hatch, farmers have to clip off part of their beaks. This keeps turkeys from pecking at each other.

Glossary

Americas North, South, and Central America

caruncle lumpy skin that grows on a turkey's neck

crop plant a farmer grows in his fields, such as corn or wheat

down small, soft, fluffy feathers that cover a chick's body

dusk time of day when the sun goes down

graze to let animals nibble or eat grass

hatch to come out of an egg

huddle to crowd together

incubate to keep eggs warm so that they hatch

lean having very little fat in the meat

national emblem something that is chosen to stand for a group of people or an idea

pellet dry food that has been mixed and formed into one piece

pen fenced-in area where animals live indoors or outside

poult very young turkey

preen to clean by gripping a feather with the beak and pulling down to the tip

raise to feed and look after young animals or children

roost to settle down to sleep

snood loose flap of skin that hangs over a turkey's beak.

starter crumb food rolled into tiny pieces

temperature how hot or cold it is

trough long, open container that holds food for animals

wattle folds of skin under a turkey's neck

yolk yellow part of an egg that is food for a turkey in its shell

More Books to Read

Cooper, Jason. *Turkeys.* Vero Beach, Fla.: Rourke Book Company, 1995.

Hill, Lee S. *Farms Feed the World.* Minneapolis: Lerner Publishing Group, 1997.

Roop, Peter, and Connie Roop. *A Farm Album.* Des Plaines, Ill.: Heinemann Library, 1998.

Index